This journal of
extraordinary
encounters
belongs to:

God Is Near: 30 Extraordinary Encounters

Copyright © 2001 Group Publishing, Inc.

Visit our Web site: www.grouppublishing.com

Credits
Contributing Writers: Jenny Baker, Steve Collins, Paul E. Gauche, and Jim Kochenburger
Editor: Kelli B. Trujillo
Creative Development Editor: Jim Kochenburger
Chief Creative Officer: Joani Schultz
Copy Editor: Janis Sampson
Art Director: Jean Bruns
Design/Illustration: Liz Howe Design
Production Manager: Dodie Tipton

Library of Congress Cataloging-in-Publication Data
God is near : 30 extraordinary encounters.
        p. cm.
    ISBN 0-7644-2328-2
        I. Christian teenagers—Prayer-books and devotions—English. I. Group Publishing.
    BV4850 .G6593 2001
    242'.63—dc21   2001023615

Printed in Korea.
10 9 8 7 6 5 4 3 2 1   10 09 08 07 06 05 04 03 02 01

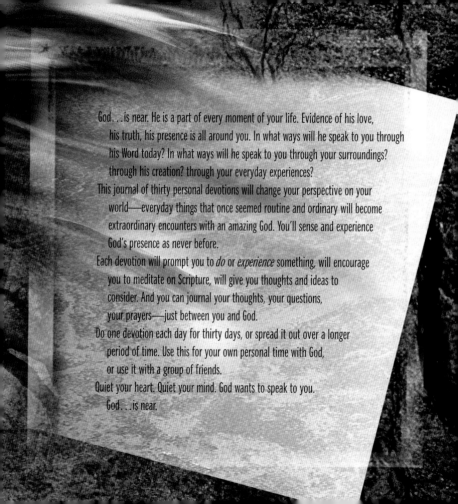

God. . .is near. He is a part of every moment of your life. Evidence of his love,
his truth, his presence is all around you. In what ways will he speak to you through
his Word today? In what ways will he speak to you through your surroundings?
through his creation? through your everyday experiences?

This journal of thirty personal devotions will change your perspective on your
world—everyday things that once seemed routine and ordinary will become
extraordinary encounters with an amazing God. You'll sense and experience
God's presence as never before.

Each devotion will prompt you to *do* or *experience* something, will encourage
you to meditate on Scripture, will give you thoughts and ideas to
consider. And you can journal your thoughts, your questions,
your prayers—just between you and God.

Do one devotion each day for thirty days, or spread it out over a longer
period of time. Use this for your own personal time with God,
or use it with a group of friends.

Quiet your heart. Quiet your mind. God wants to speak to you.
God. . .is near.

Pilgrimage

God…is near.

Stand by a busy street near where you live.

No busy street? Just stand by a road and imagine. Watch all the people rushing by in their cars. Try to see their faces…

Where do they come from?

Where are they going?

Pick out several people, focus in on them, and take a little imagination trip.

What do you think their "stories" are? (Make them up!)

Focus on one car.

Now close your eyes and imagine…You are in that car—that road is the road of life…

Read Psalm 84:1-5, 7.

Where have you come from? Where are you going? What in your life is taking you to God?

See yourself headed toward God…What could you do, think, or say to take you closer to him?

Pray.

sparrow has

How God Met Me
(Thoughts, feelings, musings, dreams, pictures, ideas...)

d a home

Windows

God...is near.

Around sunset, find a building with windows made of dark or
reflective glass. Find a place you can watch it (without
looking suspicious!). Concentrate on the reflective glass.
What happens as night falls?

Are the reflections fading? Are you starting to see through?

Can you see the light inside?

Read Matthew 17:1-2.

Jesus looked like a normal guy. His surface reflected the
surroundings...blended in.

But on the mountain, the light inside shone out in
full strength, onto his startled friends.

Think of the people you know. Do you ever see the light
of God shining through? Has anyone ever been a window
to God for you? Did you expect it? Thank God for that person.

How about you? How strong is the light inside?

How dark is the glass?

How often does the light show through?

Have you ever been a window for God? How might God shine
through you more?

All kinds of things can be windows for God's light.
Have there been times God has spoken through the world
around you? If so, thank him and treasure the memories.
If not, or not often, ask for eyes to see his presence more.
Ask him to use what's around you to shine his light into your life.

Pray.

ke the sun

How God Met Me
(Thoughts, feelings, musings, dreams,
pictures, ideas...)

Stillness

God…is near.

Go somewhere that is very noisy or simply play loud
   music in your room—*really* loud! (Warn your family
   in advance.) Play the most blaring music you can find
   ("sacred" or "secular"). As you listen, think of all the
   loudness in your life.

Think of the many voices that speak to you each day——
   the noise of the streets, the babble in the school
   hallways, the chatting in the church foyer, the
   small talk in the mall, the excited voices of friends,
   the noise of so many conflicting thoughts,
   competing attitudes, deep desires.

Now turn off the music or leave the loud
   place you've found.

Sit quietly…wait…be patient…slow down…
   let the silence sweep over you…settle your soul.

Read Psalm 46:10a aloud. Repeat it aloud. Repeat it again.

Ask God to speak to you in this place.

(wait…wait…wait…)

God speaks. Be still—he is speaking.

God is always speaking in his universe. He can speak
   to you—you can hear him.

Listen carefully…thirst for his voice…
   close your eyes…listen.

Be still…know…

Pray.

How God Met Me
(Thoughts, feelings, musings, dreams, pictures, ideas...)

A Great Light

God . . . is near.

Sit in your closet or in another small, dark place with a flashlight.

Turn on the flashlight to read the next two sentences.

Think of all the memories you have of darkness—perhaps times when
    you've been afraid, watched a scary movie in the dark, felt "dark," had a fun
      time with friends (maybe as a kid playing Capture the Flag) in the dark.

Turn off the flashlight, and think about those times for a while, then turn the light back on.

Read Isaiah 9:2-6.

Read verses 2 and 6 again.

Jesus is described here as the light. How has he been the light for you?

How have you experienced him as your light?

Has he caused you to see things differently? opened your eyes?
    guided you? helped you understand life better? understand yourself better?
    made you more loving? caused you to feel more loved?

Close your eyes and ask God to help you experience
    his light even more deeply—
    listen carefully for God to speak to you.
    Ask him to open your eyes to see what
    he wants you to see about him . . .
    about you . . .
    about his light in your life.

Pray.

How God Met Me
(Thoughts, feelings, musings, dreams, pictures, ideas...)

as document

Starry Night

God...is near.

Wait for a cloudless night.

Take a blanket and go outside to see the stars.

Lie on your back on the blanket and look up at the starry night.

Let your eyes become accustomed to the darkness—
how many stars can you see?!
(If you can't see any stars from your house,
use a flashlight to look through pictures
of the stars and planets in an
astronomy book from the library.)

Think of the distance between you and those stars.

Consider the time it takes for the light to get to you.

Imagine the planets, the moons, the galaxies around you. Think of how
much of the universe is unseen, of how far it stretches.

And think of your place in this huge cosmos. You are one person, on one blanket,
on a unique planet, under a vast expanse of sky, surrounded by millions and millions of stars.

How tiny do you feel?

Read Psalm 8:3-9.

You may be a tiny speck in a vast universe, but you are not insignificant.

God created you.

God invests in you.

God trusts you to be part of his plan.

Take time to realize your significance—to adjust your view of yourself from minuscule and unnoticed to
immensely valuable and seen by God.

In the midst of all these stars, God sees and knows and loves...you.

Pray.

e mindful of him?

Memories

God. . .is near.

Find a photo album that has pictures of you as
a young child. Choose a comfortable chair,
sit back, and look through the album. Look into
the eyes of the child that you were.

What do you feel as you look through these photos?
Are you glad you've gotten older, or do you wish you were still little?

Count the smiles that you see.

What memories do these pictures bring to mind? Are there events recorded here that you
had forgotten? Or maybe there are some moments here you would rather forget.

What is God's place in these pictures and in your memories?

Think back to your own memories in between these pictures.
How much of the past do you remember? How much of the detail of
your life has been lost?

Read Isaiah 49:15-16.

God will never forget any detail of your life.

He has been with you through everything
you have experienced.

You are so precious to him that he carries a
reminder of you on the palms of his hands.

You are remembered. You are treasured.

Can you recall times you felt as though God
was not there? Tell God about them.

Ask him to show you how he was with you
during those times.

Read the verses again and hear God speak
these words to you.

Pray.

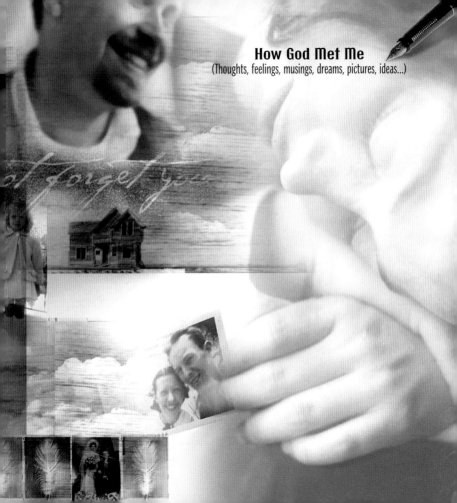

How God Met Me
(Thoughts, feelings, musings, dreams, pictures, ideas...)

Reflection

God...is near.

Look in the mirror as you get ready to go out.
   Watch yourself brushing your teeth, or fixing your
   hair, or putting on your makeup.

Do you like what you see?

Some people take ages to get ready in the morning. Others
   rush to run a comb through their hair,
   and then they're gone. What do you do?

All of us like to feel that we look OK when we face
   the rest of the world. What else do you do to make
   sure people see what you want them to see?

What masks or labels do you hide behind?
   cool? sophisticated? fun?

What blemishes do you try to cover up?

What would you change about yourself—
   inside and out? What is the *real you* like?
   How many people have met the real you?

Read Psalm 139:13-16.

You are fearfully and wonderfully made—
   this is truth.

God looks at you and admires his handiwork.

Can you do the same?

Stand tall, look yourself in the eye,
   smile back at your reflection, and thank God for the
   good job he has done in creating you.

Pray.

onderfully made

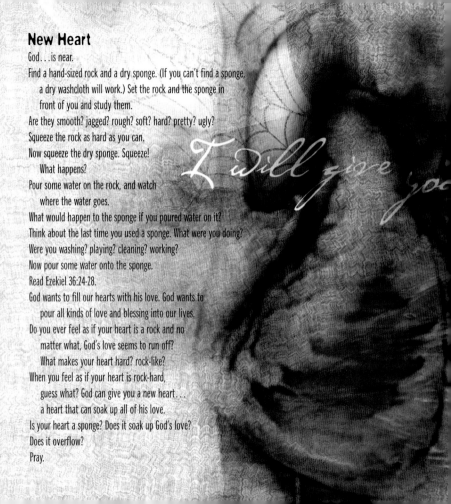

New Heart

God...is near.

Find a hand-sized rock and a dry sponge. (If you can't find a sponge,
a dry washcloth will work.) Set the rock and the sponge in
front of you and study them.

Are they smooth? jagged? rough? soft? hard? pretty? ugly?

Squeeze the rock as hard as you can.

Now squeeze the dry sponge. Squeeze!
What happens?

Pour some water on the rock, and watch
where the water goes.

What would happen to the sponge if you poured water on it?

Think about the last time you used a sponge. What were you doing?

Were you washing? playing? cleaning? working?

Now pour some water onto the sponge.

Read Ezekiel 36:24-28.

God wants to fill our hearts with his love. God wants to
pour all kinds of love and blessing into our lives.

Do you ever feel as if your heart is a rock and no
matter what, God's love seems to run off?
What makes your heart hard? rock-like?

When you feel as if your heart is rock-hard,
guess what? God can give you a new heart...
a heart that can soak up all of his love.

Is your heart a sponge? Does it soak up God's love?

Does it overflow?

Pray.

new heart

How God Met Me
(Thoughts, feelings,
musings, dreams, pictures, ideas...)

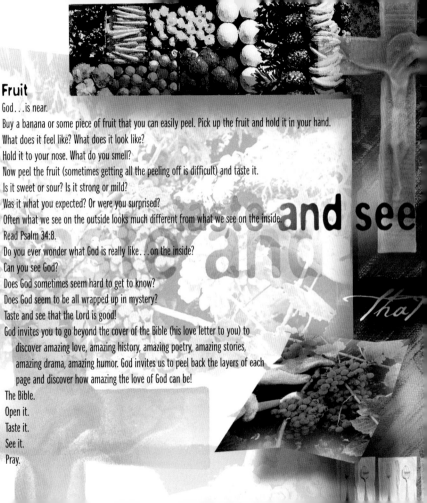

Fruit

God...is near.

Buy a banana or some piece of fruit that you can easily peel. Pick up the fruit and hold it in your hand.

What does it feel like? What does it look like?

Hold it to your nose. What do you smell?

Now peel the fruit (sometimes getting all the peeling off is difficult) and taste it.

Is it sweet or sour? Is it strong or mild?

Was it what you expected? Or were you surprised?

Often what we see on the outside looks much different from what we see on the inside.

Read Psalm 34:8.

Do you ever wonder what God is really like...on the inside?

Can you see God?

Does God sometimes seem hard to get to know?

Does God seem to be all wrapped up in mystery?

Taste and see that the Lord is good!

God invites you to go beyond the cover of the Bible (his love letter to you) to
discover amazing love, amazing history, amazing poetry, amazing stories,
amazing drama, amazing humor. God invites us to peel back the layers of each
page and discover how amazing the love of God can be!

The Bible.

Open it.

Taste it.

See it.

Pray.

How God Met Me
(Thoughts, feelings, musings, dreams, pictures, ideas...)

taste and see

the Lord is good

Maps

God. . .is near.

Find a map of your city and locate your street. Think about all of the people who live close to you and in the neighborhoods around you.

Now imagine that you're on a vacation. With your finger, follow along all of the roads that lead you away from your home. Then trace your finger back. Think about all of the people whose homes you would pass as you traced those roads.

What do you think it's like on those roads right now?

Think about what you might find along the way:

stop signs. . .detours. . .lakes. . .
closed roads. . .parked cars.

How far from your home have you been?

Have you ever been lost? Have you ever felt all alone?

Have you ever felt like you needed some direction in your life?

Did you find your own way back or did someone rescue you?

What was it like to come home again?

Read Luke 15:11-24.

Sometimes we feel very far away from God.

But God is always near.

Put your finger back on the map—
on your geographical home.

Where is your spiritual home?

Imagine God saying to you, "Welcome home!"

Say to yourself, "I am home."

Say out loud, "I am at home with God."

Pray.

...he was lost

is found.

How God Met Me
(Thoughts, feelings, musings, dreams, pictures, ideas...)

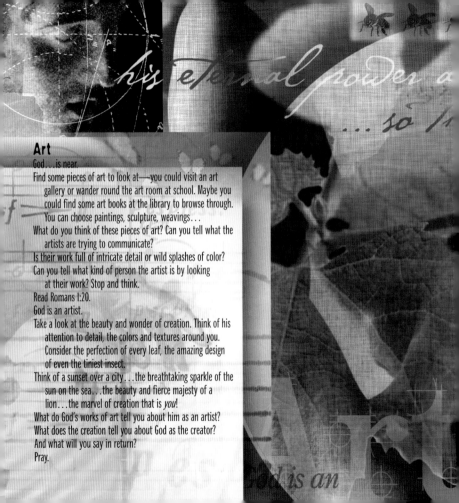

Art

God...is near.

Find some pieces of art to look at—you could visit an art
gallery or wander round the art room at school. Maybe you
could find some art books at the library to browse through.
You can choose paintings, sculpture, weavings...

What do you think of these pieces of art? Can you tell what the
artists are trying to communicate?

Is their work full of intricate detail or wild splashes of color?

Can you tell what kind of person the artist is by looking
at their work? Stop and think.

Read Romans 1:20.

God is an artist.

Take a look at the beauty and wonder of creation. Think of his
attention to detail, the colors and textures around you.
Consider the perfection of every leaf, the amazing design
of even the tiniest insect.

Think of a sunset over a city...the breathtaking sparkle of the
sun on the sea...the beauty and fierce majesty of a
lion...the marvel of creation that is *you*!

What do God's works of art tell you about him as an artist?

What does the creation tell you about God as the creator?

And what will you say in return?

Pray.

God is an

divine nature...

men are without excuse

...what will you say in return?

How God Met Me
(Thoughts, feelings, musings, dreams, pictures, ideas...)

Seasons

God...is near.

Find a large tree and sit under it.

Breathe deeply and look up through the branches. Enjoy the size and
strength of the tree.

Find a leaf and look closely at it. Think of the different seasons of the year.
Imagine how this tree looks in each of those seasons. Think of the
changes to the leaves throughout the year.

What season is it now? What will happen next to the tree?

Often we go through seasons in our spiritual lives...

Summer...We feel close to God, warm in his love, growing, and bearing fruit.

Fall...It feels as if things are dying, it's getting colder.

Winter...There's little sign of life, God may feel distant.

Spring...There are new buds and signs of hope, God is moving...
It's a time of promise.

Which spiritual season are you in?

Read Genesis 8:22.

Year after year the seasons follow one another—a sign of God's
faithfulness to his people. Spring *always* follows winter—
nothing will stop that as long as the earth endures.

Just as God maintains the rhythms of the year, he will be
faithful to you. He is with you now and will lead you on.

Thank God for the spiritual season you are in, and tell him
how you feel about it. Thank him for what's ahead.

Will you walk with God and trust him?

Pray.

summer and winter,

day and night

will never cease

eedtime and harvest,

cold and heat,

it endures,

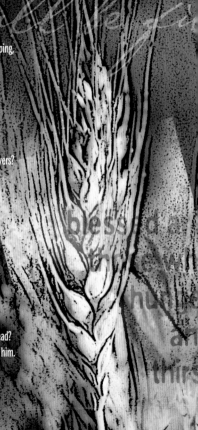

Hunger

God...is near.

Sit in the kitchen and watch someone preparing a meal for you
    (or prepare one for yourself).

Consider the work that goes into this meal—the measuring, the chopping,
    the stirring, and the baking.

Savor the smells and the warmth of the kitchen. Anticipate the tastes
    that you will soon enjoy.

Are you hungry? Will you be able to wait...or are you
    tempted to sneak a taste before it's ready?

Think about your spiritual life. Are you hungry for more of God?
    Are you waiting for him to fulfill your longing, to answer your prayers?

Or have you filled yourself up with busyness and spent so much
    time on other things that you have forgotten
    what it's like to hunger for God?

Read Matthew 5:3-10.

Those who hunger and thirst will be filled.

If you hunger, does it seem that satisfaction is a long time coming?
    That hunger will overwhelm you? Are you tempted to try
    something else to satisfy your spiritual longing?

Eating before a meal takes the edge off your hunger,
    but means you don't fully appreciate the meal and it is spoiled.

    If you aren't hungry for God, what have you been feeding on instead?

    Talk to God about it, and ask him to help you wait and hunger for him.

Hold on to his promise and ask him to satisfy your hunger.

Pray.

...ssed are the poor in spirit,
or theirs is the kingdom of heaven.
...ssed are those who mourn,
...or they will be comforted.
...sed are the meek,
...or they will inherit the earth.
...ssed are those who hunger and thirst for righte...
...or they will be filled.
...ssed are the merciful,
...or they will be shown mercy.
...ssed are the pure in heart,
...or they will see God.
...ssed are the peacemakers,
...for they will be called sons of God.
...ssed are those who are persecuted because...
...for theirs is the kingdom of heaven.

How God Met Me
(Thoughts, feelings, musings,
dreams, pictures, ideas...)

Forgiveness

God . . . is near.

Find some open water—a lake, a river, a pond, or a deep
  puddle. If there is no open water near you, sit outside and
  fill a big bucket with water. Imagine it's a deep, deep lake.

Pick up a stone and brush off the dirt. Dip it into the water,
  and wash it clean. How does the stone look and
  feel with the dust and dirt rinsed away?

Now think about your life and the "dust and dirt"
  you may have picked up today. What is it like to
  try to clean your inner self?

Hold the stone in your hand. Ask God to show you where
  you need to be cleansed:
    maybe for things you have said . . .
    or for things you have done . . .
    perhaps for your thoughts . . .

Talk to God about these things and ask him to forgive you.
  Take your time.

Imagine these things wrapped around the stone in
  your hand. Now throw the stone into the water—
  as high, as far as you can.

Watch it splash and disappear.

Watch the ripples fade away.

Read Psalm 103:11-12.

Can you get your stone back? Do you want to?

That's how God treats forgiven sin—
  it's gone, it's forgotten, it's not to be retrieved.

Close your eyes, breathe deeply, and savor the
  cleansing of God's forgiveness.

Rejoice that God has made you pure.

Thank God for his forgiveness . . .
  and make sure you forgive yourself.

Pray.

How God Met Me
(Thoughts, feelings, musings, dreams, pictures, ideas...)

Running

God...is near.

Go for a run. Run as far as you can.

Pay attention to your body. When you feel exhausted, keep running until you just *can't* run anymore. Find a place to be alone.

Why did you run? Why did you keep going even when you were weary?

Did you enjoy the run? Why? Why not?

What are some things you do in your spiritual life that are like running—activities you do to experience and feel close to God, but which can sometimes become routine and simply make you weary?

How do you keep going when you are weary of spiritual running? Are you enjoying your spiritual running?

Read Isaiah 40:28-31.

God wants you to enjoy your spiritual life. God doesn't want you to become weary or for it ever to become boring. He wants you to be strengthened and renewed. He wants you to feel you are running well—he wants you to feel like a winner, not a loser.

Hold your hands in victory above your head...close your eyes...breathe in and out deeply...picture God filling you with strength...filling you with encouragement... with joy in a race well run...with a reminder that it is for him and to him you run...breathe in and out deeply...

Pray.

How God Met Me
(Thoughts, feelings, musings, dreams, pictures, ideas...)

Strength

God...is near.

Go try to lift something you would not normally think you could lift, like a car or a heavy rock. Try to lift it or carry it using only your hands, arms, or back. (Don't hurt yourself!)

...Keep trying...

Think of the strongest people you know as you lift. Try to lift the item again each time you think of someone.

Think of Superman and try to lift again.

What types of things do those people who are strong try to lift?

What are some things even the strongest person can't lift?

Now close your eyes and think of you...

What kinds of heavy things are you trying to lift or carry alone in your life—not physically, but emotionally? spiritually?

Read I Peter 5:6-7.

God wants to help you carry that weight. Take time to think of each problem, challenge, or relationship tension you need God's help to "lift" and "carry."

See God lifting and carrying for you each thing that comes to mind...

Rest...

Let the Lord lift...

Let him carry...

He loves you...His finger can move mountains...His arm can hold up the universe...His eyes can see right into the deepest places of your heart.

He sees what you are carrying alone...Let him carry it...

Pray.

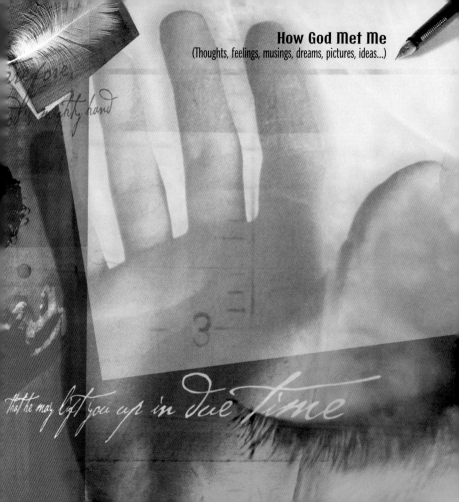

How God Met Me
(Thoughts, feelings, musings, dreams, pictures, ideas...)

that he may lift you up in due time

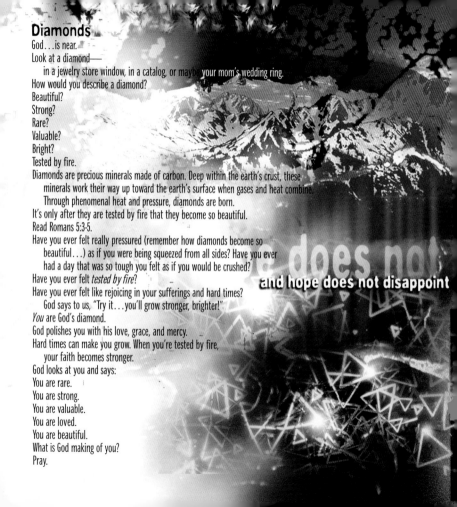

Diamonds

God...is near.

Look at a diamond—

    in a jewelry store window, in a catalog, or maybe your mom's wedding ring.

How would you describe a diamond?

Beautiful?

Strong?

Rare?

Valuable?

Bright?

Tested by fire.

Diamonds are precious minerals made of carbon. Deep within the earth's crust, these

    minerals work their way up toward the earth's surface when gases and heat combine.

    Through phenomenal heat and pressure, diamonds are born.

It's only after they are tested by fire that they become so beautiful.

Read Romans 5:3-5.

Have you ever felt really pressured (remember how diamonds become so

    beautiful...) as if you were being squeezed from all sides? Have you ever

    had a day that was so tough you felt as if you would be crushed?

Have you ever felt *tested by fire*?

Have you ever felt like rejoicing in your sufferings and hard times?

    God says to us, "Try it...you'll grow stronger, brighter!"

You are God's diamond.

God polishes you with his love, grace, and mercy.

Hard times can make you grow. When you're tested by fire,

    your faith becomes stronger.

God looks at you and says:

You are rare.

You are strong.

You are valuable.

You are loved.

You are beautiful.

What is God making of you?

Pray.

and hope does not disappoint

How God Met Me
(Thoughts, feelings, musings,
dreams, pictures, ideas...)

appoint us

Money

God...is near.

Empty out your wallet, and put all
   your money in a pile.

Spend some time looking at it, feeling it, smelling it.

Imagine how many different wallets, pockets,
   cash registers, and banks this money has passed
   through. Think about what it might have
   been used to buy.

Perhaps one person bought luxuries like diamonds or
   champagne...another bought basics
   like diapers and milk.

Some people may have treasured this money.
   Some may have taken it for granted.

What about you? How will you use this money?
   How do you feel about money?

Do you wish you had more, or are you content?

Read Proverbs 30:8-9.

Having too much money, or too little,
   can make it harder to worship God.

Where are you? With too much, too little,
   or just enough?

God promises to give us our daily bread...
   enough for each day...all that we need.

Will you trust him to provide you with your daily bread?

Are you content to let God decide what is enough?

Tell God how you feel about money...
   ask him to provide for you.

Pray.

poverty nor riches

How God Met Me
(Thoughts, feelings, musings, dreams, pictures, ideas...)

30:8-9

Keep falsehood and lies far from me;
give me neither poverty nor riches,
but give me only my daily bread.
Otherwise, I may have too much and
and say, 'Who is the LORD?'
Or I may become poor and steal,
and so dishonor the name of my God

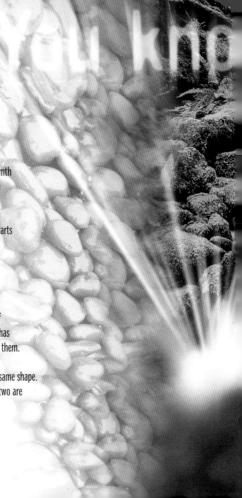

Pebble

God . . . is near.

Find a pebble, small enough to close your hand around.

> Put it in your pocket and turn it in your hand.
>
> Explore its surface with your fingers. What shape is it?
>
> Is it rough or smooth? Or both in different places?

Read Psalm 139:1-5, 23-24.

Like the pebble, you are unique. God holds you in the warmth
of his hand, turning you gently, searching your surface
for flaws and rough places. Where do you think those
flaws might be? Ask God to show you and to help you
offer them to him. Where are the smooth places, the parts
that are pleasing to God's touch? Ask God to show you
and to help you offer them to him.

Still ponds don't make pebbles—it takes moving water,
like a river or the sea. The water takes the rock on
a journey and wears it smooth by rubbing it against
other rocks. How far have you traveled in the water of
the Spirit? Think about the people and situations God has
used to smooth your sharp edges, and give thanks for them.

How willing are you to be made a different shape?

> Sometimes we fear that God will make us all into the same shape.
> Take the pebble out of your pocket and look at it. No two are
> the same.

Pray.

How God Met Me
(Thoughts, feelings, musings, dreams,
pictures, ideas...)

Like a Child

God...is near.

If you can, run a sprinkler outside. Stand under it and run through it.
(Place this book inside a plastic bag so you can take it with you.)
If you can't set up a sprinkler, simply go take a shower, but run
the water a little cool (to get the "sprinkler in the yard" effect).
Enjoy the water for a while. Let it flow and fall all over you.

What is your favorite childhood memory of water or playing in
a sprinkler? swimming?

In what ways do you still feel like a child?

Do you laugh easily? play and goof around? Is everything serious,
or do you still cut loose? When were you silly most recently?

Think of the last time your curiosity overcame you...
Do you wonder about things? experience awe? think new ideas?
wish for simple, happy endings?

Read Luke 18:15-17.

You are God's precious child, deeply loved
and uniquely crafted by him—inside and out.
In certain ways he designed you to grow and
in other ways to stay forever young.

How does he want you to grow?

How does he want you to stay forever young?

How would your life be different if you were more childlike?

Pray.

like a little child enter it

How God Met Me
(Thoughts, feelings,
musings, dreams, pictures, ideas...)

Cleaning Up

God...is near.

Go to a place in your room
  you haven't cleaned up for a while.
  Could be a closet, under the bed...
  the whole room! Take everything out,
  and sort it into some kind of order—
  things of the same kind, things that aren't
  the same but go together, things to throw away,
  things you're not sure about.

Read Luke 15:8-10.

Have you found anything you loved but thought you'd lost?
  How long was it missing? Did you ever notice it was missing
  and search for it?

As you put the things that are important in safe places, think about God.
  Do you ever lose touch with him? How hard do you search?
  Are you delighted when you find him?

Look at the stuff that hid the things you value. What are the things in your life that hide God?
  What buries the kingdom and makes you forget? Some of those
  things you can keep, but they will need to be put where
  they aren't in the way of what really matters.

Maybe some stuff has to go. Some of those decisions are easy, some hard.
  When you've finished cleaning up, ask God what needs
  cleaning up inside you. God may see value in things you
  thought were worthless, or he may want you to get
  rid of something you wanted to hoard.

Pray.

How God Met Me
(Thoughts, feelings, musings, dreams, pictures, ideas...)

sinner who repents

The eye is T...

Glasses

God...is near.

How good is your eyesight? Is it twenty-twenty,
or do you have to wear glasses?

If you are wearing them now, take them off.
Can you still read this? Whether you need glasses or not,
borrow someone else's. How do things look? Can you read?
Can you walk straight?

If you can, borrow more than one pair of glasses to look
through. How do they differ? Can you find two
pairs the same? What does this tell you about the owners?

Read Matthew 6:22-23.

How good is your inner eyesight? How do you see the world?
Do you look for good or evil?

Do you see black and white, shades of gray, or sixteen
million colors? Think about where your soul gets its
"glasses." Are they from God? If not, where are they from?
your friends? yourself? the world? Do they color
what's inside you?

Are there things that distort your vision? Ask God for
healing or for help to leave those things behind.

Are there things in your life that help you see true?
Thank God for them, and wear those "glasses" as
much as you can.

Pray.

amp of the body

Just a Reminder

God...is near.

Find an alarm clock, and set it to ring or
  buzz in the next five to ten minutes. Now
  lay down and wait for the alarm to go off.
  While you're resting, think about what
  alarms remind you to do:

Wake up.

Get up.

Get out.

Start something.

Finish something.

Be somewhere.

Alarms remind us to do important things. When was the last time an alarm went off for you?

What did you do?

Did you shut off the alarm and go back to sleep, or did you do what the alarm reminded you to do?

Read Luke 17:11-19.

Only one out of ten remembered to thank Jesus. One out of ten...
  Are you like that *one*? Do you need a reminder to thank God?

For life...for friends...for family...for joys...
  for challenges...for his awesome love and amazing grace.

What are you truly thankful for today?

Before the alarm goes off, think of ten things that you are thankful for—tell God thanks.

What are some things in your life that can be "alarms" for you—
  to remind you to thank God?

Do you need reminders?
  They're all around you.

When the alarm sounds, turn it off...
  close your eyes...spend some time with God.

Pray.

wake up

get up

get out

start something

finish something

be somewhere

How God Met Me
(Thoughts, feelings, musings, dreams, pictures, ideas...)

Compass

God...is near.

Stand outside your home holding a stiff piece of paper or cardboard. Place a compass on it.

Let the needle stabilize, then draw an arrow pointing in the same direction. If you can't find
a compass, you can use the sun by holding the pen upright on the page to make a shadow.

Read Psalm 25:4-10.

Go for a walk. Every time you take a turn, hold the paper the same way and draw an arrow pointing
in the direction of the compass needle or shadow of the sun. For a moment,
turn to face in the direction the needle is pointing.
How does it relate to the way you're heading now?
Are the directions ever the same?

The path of following God is as consistent as the compass needle.
It always goes the same way, whatever direction that
might look like in comparison to our lives.

How often have you been
heading in the direction
that God points?

Are you heading that way now?
If not, why? Talk to God about it,
and ask him to teach you his paths.

When you get home, look at the arrows you've drawn.
Do any of them point the same way?
Who changed direction: you or the compass needle?

Do you find God's path easy to walk in? Is it easy to find?
If you feel you have lost direction, ask God to guide you.

Pray.

How God Met Me
(Thoughts, feelings, musings,
dreams, pictures, ideas...)

Clothing

God...is near.

Go to the mall or a shopping center
(or close your eyes, relax, and think
back to your last trip there).

Watch the people buying clothing—
pay attention to what they are
wearing, how they are walking. Note
the body language. Note the attitudes.

Are you really seeing people?

Seeing who they *really* are?

Go into a clothing store and browse. Listen to the
conversations of other shoppers. What kinds of
clothing are they looking for? Why?

What might they hope the clothing will do for them?

Find a place to be alone.

Think about this for a moment:

What's your favorite outfit? Why?

How do clothes make you what you are or define
your image to others?

Now think of God...what is the coolest thing about him?

Read Colossians 3:12-14.

Think of God as a garment, something you put on.

How are you "wearing" God in your life?

How does he define your image to others?

Is he a big part of who you are?

How would you like to "wear" God
even more in your life?

Pray.

clothe yourselves with compassion

put on love

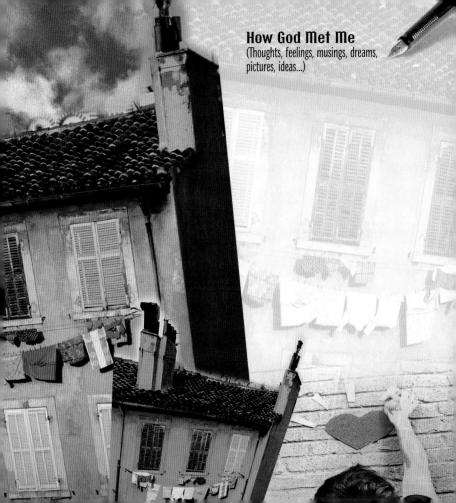

How God Met Me
(Thoughts, feelings, musings, dreams, pictures, ideas...)

Mail

God . . . is near.

Go and pick up your mail.

Before you open it, look at the
different sizes, shapes, colors.

Which is the largest item? the smallest?
Which looks most appealing?
least appealing? Which envelopes
tell you about their contents?
Which give no clue?

Do you recognize anything? If so, are you
pleased to see it or not? Why?

Now start opening. How do you decide what to open first?
How easy are the envelopes to open?
How different are the contents from the appearance
of the envelope? Is it what you expected or
are you surprised? Is the surprise good or bad?

Was there anything missing? mail you have been waiting
for that didn't arrive? How long have you waited,
and why? If it came today, how did you feel?

Read 2 Corinthians 3:2-3.

What kind of letter from God are you?

Are you a love letter or a demand for payment?

Does your envelope give a clue to the contents?
How easy is it to open? Who could be waiting for
the message? Is there anything you need to do?

What about other people? Are they letters from God too?

How can you tell?

Has anyone been a letter from God to you?
What kind of letter? Were you surprised?
How ready are you to receive?
How ready are you to give?

Pray.

How God Met Me
(Thoughts, feelings, musings, dreams, pictures, ideas...)

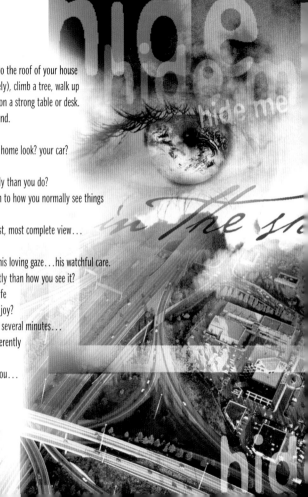

Perspective

God. . .is near.

Go to the highest place you can—to the roof of your house
(this is best *if* you can do it safely), climb a tree, walk up
a hill, sit high on a chair, stand on a strong table or desk.
Take a few minutes to look around.

Take all of it in, a bird's-eye view.

If you were a bird, how would your home look? your car?
the people below?

How would you see things differently than you do?

Compare what you see from up high to how you normally see things
on level ground.

God can see everything—the widest, most complete view. . .
He sees it all. . .all at once. . .

Nothing escapes his warm smile. . .his loving gaze. . .his watchful care.

How does God see your life differently than how you see it?

What do you think he sees in your life
right now that most brings him joy?

Dwell on all that comes to mind for several minutes. . .

How do you think God sees you differently
than you even see yourself?
(Think of his limitless love for you. . .
how much he delights in you.)

Read Psalm 17:1-8 aloud.

You are the apple of God's eye.

Pray.

How God Met Me
(Thoughts, feelings, musings, dreams, pictures, ideas...)

Salt

God...is near.

While you are having a meal, put a heap of salt on the edge of your plate. Look at its color.

Taste a little.

In what ways is it different from the food on your plate?

Taste something on your plate that isn't salty. Now sprinkle a little salt on it. What happens to the salt? Can you still see it? If not, where did it go?

Taste the food again. How is it different? What did the salt do? What did the salt lose when you put it on the food? What did it keep?

Read Matthew 5:13.

According to Jesus, what matters about salt? What does it need to keep? Is that what it kept when you put it on your food?

Salt is necessary for life.

Salt stops things from spoiling and helps heal wounds.

Salt stops you from slipping on ice.

And Jesus says you are salt...

Do you hang out on the edge of the plate?

If you asked God to sprinkle you on the world, what might you lose? What would you still have?

What difference could you make to the flavor?

Ask God if there's somewhere he wants you to get involved. When you put salt on your food, were you trying to make the food taste of nothing but salt? Or did the salt draw out the flavor? What does that mean about how you get involved in the world?

Pray.

You are the salt

Life

Each man's life is but a breath.

God…is near.

Go to a cemetery near you (or look at a picture of a graveyard). Read the many headstones.

Try to imagine the people buried there and the lives they lived.

Were they happy? sad? successful? failures?

Loved? unloved? alone? surrounded by friends?

Were their lives easy or hard? What were their dreams?

Did they achieve them?

What do you think God's purpose was for their lives?

Did they realize it?

Think about you…and God.

What do you know he has created you to be? to do?

God has a plan for you—a plan beyond your wildest dreams,

beyond your most amazing imaginings. What do you know of it so far?

Did you know that the desires deep within you,

the passions that move you deeply, the stuff you care most about,

the things in the world you most want to see changed,

the stuff that can most quickly bring a tear to your

eye or a smile, what most deeply satisfies you…

they're all things that can lead you to God's purpose for you and your life.

Read Psalm 39:4-7.

Touch the dirt or grass around a grave.

Rub it between your fingers.

When you die, what would you want your friends and family to say about your life?

What one thing would you most want to change in this world?

What one thing can make you feel satisfied or completely fulfilled in life?

Pray.

Hope is in you.

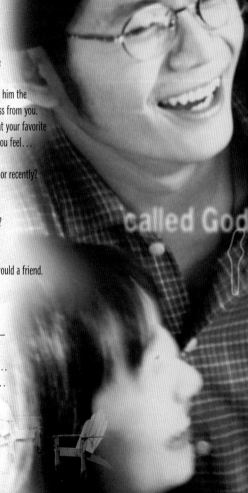

Friends

God... is near.

Serve yourself your favorite beverage (perhaps a Coke
    or coffee) and go have a chat with a friend...
      that is, God. Pull up a chair for him. In fact, serve him the
      same beverage you're drinking. Set his place across from you.
      Have a chat with God just as you would a friend at your favorite
      hangout. Have a serious or light time, whatever you feel...

What's happening in your life?

What's something funny that happened to you today or recently?

Who is that special someone in your life? Why?

What has been most on your mind?

Are you feeling up or down lately? Why, do you think?

How's it going with Mom or Dad?

What's the latest news on everything and everybody?

Don't hold anything back... just talk to God as you would a friend.

Read James 2:23.

... called God's friend...

God is your friend. The best friend you'll ever have.

He's the only one who knows everything about you—
    the number of hairs on your head...
      every attitude... every thought... every feeling...
      every care... every trouble... every good thing...
      every really cool thing happening in your life...
      and he loves you perfectly and unconditionally.

How do you treat God as a friend?

Pray.

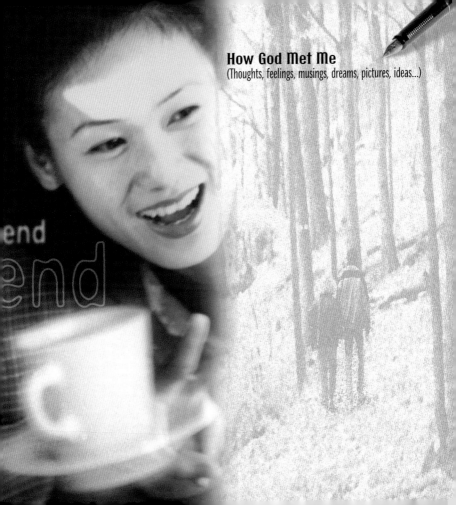

How God Met Me
(Thoughts, feelings, musings, dreams, pictures, ideas...)

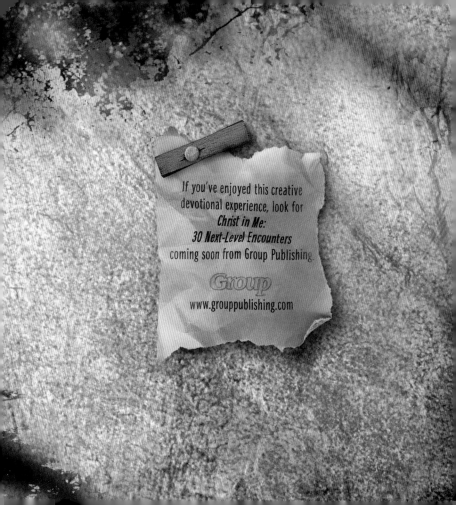